# HANUMAN CHALISA
## Leap of Faith
### Essence and Sanskrit Grammar

Ashwini Kumar Aggarwal

जय गुरुदेव

Title: **Hanuman Chalisa Leap of Faith**
SubTitle: **Essence and Sanskrit Grammar**
Author: **Ashwini Kumar Aggarwal**

Printed and Published by
**Devotees of Sri Sri Ravi Shankar Ashram**
34 Sunny Enclave, Devigarh Road,
Patiala 147001, Punjab, India

https://advaita56.in/
The Art of Living Centre
https://www.artofliving.org/

14th July 2023, Shravana Krishna Dvadashi, Rohini
Nakshatra, Varsha Ritu, Uttarayana. Pradosh Vrat.

Yesterday ISRO scientists offered prayers at Tirupati Venkatachalapathy
Temple, with a miniature model. Today Chandrayaan-3 consisting of
Propulsion Module, Moon Lander and Rover launched by LVM3-M4 Rocket
at 2:35pm IST from Satish Dhawan Space Centre, Sriharikota.

Vikram Samvat 2080 Pingala, Saka Era 1945 Shobhakrit

1st Edition July 2023

जय गुरुदेव

# Dedication

## Sri Sri Ravi Shankar

who taught us to worship, to pray, to sing and chant

# Acknowledgements

The fantastic books, Illustrated Ramayana and Mahabharata published by Dorling Kindersley DK's amazing team.

# Front Cover Photo Credits

Black granite statue. Photo by MikeGz from Pexels: https://www.pexels.com/photo/statue-of-hanuman-hindu-god-15239045/

# Blessing

Only one who is strong can surrender.

Sri Sri Ravi Shankar

https://twitter.com/SriSri/status/1639671954901958656

Hanuman Chalisa Rajasthani Miniature Painting

# Preface

The Hanuman Chalisa is chanted and sung in every Indian home.

It was composed by Goswami Tulsidas, the author of Ramcharitmanas fame, circa 16$^{th}$ century CE.

It is a prayer to Strength-Valor-Faith.
It is that which brings up and nurtures these qualities.

∞ ∞ ∞

I first read about Hanuman when I was 5 years old. It was a small book in Hindi, and it captured my imagination totally.

It was the year 2011-2012, when Sri Sri first asked us to sing the Hanuman Chalisa in Vishalakshi Mantap, Bangalore Ashram.

Honey Dew Drop Hema has had the Divine darshan of Hanuman ever since she was in 2$^{nd}$ standard.

# Contents

श्री हनूमते नमः ॥ ॐ हं हनूमते नमः ॥

śrī hanūmate namaḥ ॥ oṃ haṃ hanūmate namaḥ ॥

## ॥ श्री हनुमान चालीसा ॥  ॥ śrī hanumāna cālīsā ॥

## Prologue

॥ दोहा ॥
श्रीगुरु चरन सरोज रज
 निज मनु मुकुरु सुधारि ।
बरनउँ रघुबर बिमल जसु
 जो दायकु फल चारि ॥

॥ dohā ॥
śrīguru carana saroja raja
 nija manu mukuru sudhāri ǀ
baranauṁ raghubara bimala jasu
 jo dāyaku phala cāri ॥

No one knows. No one understands. It is a mystery. The senses and intellect grapple and give up empty handed. Yet the heart senses. It accepts. A tiny bud of faith is born.

There is a man whom they call the Master. The Guru. The one who appears like one of us, yet is in no way made up of flesh, muscles, 5 elements or anything else known to man. The Guru is an X entity. Never has he been cognized by mankind. Somewhere sometime the idea of God sprang up. Anything unknown was labelled as God, when it became known it lost its tag. As man evolved, he came no closer to

God than his ancestors. Man made brilliant discoveries and inventions, he built splendid cities and cutting edge communication channels, however God remained elusive, not an inch closer.

It worried the pundits and scholars. It became unbearable for the philosophers and thinkers. Finally, someone at some point in time coined the word Guru. Master. Suddenly God was there. Available. Transactable. Wishes got Fulfilled. Victories got achieved. Impossible was made possible, darned simple. God materialized out of nowhere just by this simple word "Guru". God took the form of Guru. And life began to get cheerful, exciting, fascinating. Man started to dream. He started to play and laugh and have fun. Families got strengthened, societies got infused with love, planet Earth finally began to be noticed in the superstructure of the cosmos, the galactic emperors visited and paid their obeisance.

For all ye newborns, teenagers, raw and green gentlemen and lassies. Before you eat, before you go out, before you speak, bring to mind this word GURU. Attach to it SHRI. And with respect, faith and a sense of belongingness begin your day, step out into the sunshine, utter whatever your throat cannot hold any longer.

Just tell the mind that the Guru is the one whose friendship, whose closeness, whose interactions shall make my mind brilliant like a spotless mirror which shows every detail. When by Guru's presence my mind becomes glistening and bright, I take firm, bold, and pragmatic steps towards success. I qualify to achieve the greatness and centeredness of Lord Rama. In fact, that is my first priority, that is my life's aim, to reach the heights attained by the finest human being born in the family of Raghu, a brave king of ancient India. I too wish to lead the life that Shri Rama lived, I too wish to be the beloved of mother Earth, and earn the respect of all. That is what has been stated by the Vedas as the 4 endeavors of a complete man - Dharma Artha Kama Moksha.

Dharma - expression of my essential nature, genetic drive, temperament, and core design.

Artha - earning sufficient wealth that can achieve big tasks related to entire nation and make a legendary impact in the lives of millions.

Kama - having utmost passion in my work and my responsibility, thereby enjoying real filial bliss and exciting entertainment.

Moksha - strong undercurrent of God's presence, intuition, and gut feeling, that keeps me anchored in peace within and steers me beautifully through life.

बुद्धिहीन तनु जानिके

सुमिरौं पवनकुमार ।

बल बुधि बिद्या देहु मोहिं

हरहु कलेस बिकार ॥

buddhihīna tanu jānike

sumiraum pavanakumāra |

bala budhi bidyā dehu mohim

harahu kalesa bikāra ||

Knowing that my infinitesimal intellect is always alert and alive due to the Lord's presence in the form of Prana Vayu, the vital air coursing through my body, I feel encouraged and strengthened to have big targets and aim for the stars. Since my intellect knows that my body shall be well taken care of, my family shall have all comforts and safety, I go forth boldly on my mission to surmount herculean challenges and achieve magnificent targets.

16th century Madhava Ranga temple Hampi, Karnataka

# The Leap



## 1 Pure Oxygen Breath

जय हनुमान ज्ञान गुण सागर ।

जय कपीस तिहुँ लोक उजागर ॥ १

jaya hanumāna jñāna guṇa sāgara |

jaya kapīsa tihuṁ loka ujāgara ‖ 1

Hail o Breath, hail ye Pana, victory to thee Vital air coursing through my veins and filling my lungs and making me feel invincible. This rich nourishing pure oxygen makes my brain function to peak performance, infusing me with an effulgent intellect that takes clear decisions. My broad vision and well informed decisions light up the whole world and show the path to innumerable souls.

## 2 Father speedy Wind, Mother caring Anjani

राम दूत अतुलित बल धामा ।

अंजनिपुत्र पवनसुत नामा ॥ २

rāma dūta atulita bala dhāmā |

aṁjaniputra pavanasuta nāmā ‖ 2

The noble Lord Rama is pleased and gives me his impeccable darshan. My mother Anjani's heart fills up with pride and showers me with untold blessings. The Lord of seasons, weather, climate, and currents, named Pavan, (Vayu or the Wind-God) is overjoyed at my exploits and addresses me as his dear son.

## 3 Birth of Faith

महाबीर बिक्रम बजरंगी ।

कुमति निवार सुमति के संगी ॥ ३

mahābīra bikrama bajaraṃgī |

kumati nivāra sumati ke saṃgī ॥ 3

Faith is born. Faith is strengthened. Faith becomes the springboard for leaping towards the stars. Any weakness in me gets erased, All virtues in me blossom.

## 4 Skin Tone Golden Sunset

कंचन बरन बिराज सुबेसा ।

कानन कुंडल कुंचित केसा ॥ ४

kaṃcana barana birāja subesā |

kānana kuṃḍala kuṃcita kesā ॥ 4

The skin matches the tone of the golden sunlight, the apparel is of the finest silk and cotton. My ears resound with the names of the eternal Lord, my ego melts and becomes the road, nay the soft cushion for the Lord's lotus feet.

## 5 Flag of Enthusiasm

हाथ बज्र औ ध्वजा बिराजै ।

काँधे मूँज जनेऊ साजै ॥ ५

hātha bajra au dhvajā birājai |

kāṃdhe mūṃja janeū sājai ॥ 5

The flag of enthusiasm and happiness heralds my arrival,

the mace of solidity and integrity stamps my faith. The bond of acceptance and belongingness brings us all together.

Auspiciousness showers wherever we go, the saffron color is sprinkled signifying good health for all. Smiling faces looking out of each window, the divine air gushes into each home to ensure long term stability and amicability.

## 6 Doors of Wisdom

संकर सुवन केसरी नंदन ।

तेज प्रताप महा जग बंदन ॥ ६

saṃkara suvana kesarī naṃdana |

teja pratāpa mahā jaga baṃdana || 6

Even the doors of wisdom are thrown wide open, and folks' talents bloom in each others' Satsang presence.

Hanuman helping Lord Ram build the Ram Setu bridge in the Treta Yuga, from Rameswaram India to Mannar Sri Lanka.

## 7 Lord's Longing

बिद्यावान गुणी अति चातुर ।

राम काज करिबे को आतुर ॥ ७

bidyāvāna guṇī ati cātura |

rāma kāja karibe ko ātura ‖ 7

The ambience brims with devotees longing for the Lord's darshan, and hoping to get involved In creative infrastructure building projects that uplift society.

Many folks participate in singing divine songs and worshipping the divine by relating the Lord's leela, and making art and architecture that reflects the Lord's beauty.


## 8 Ram Sita Laxman

प्रभु चरित्र सुनिबे को रसिया ।

राम लखन सीता मन बसिया ॥ ८

prabhu caritra sunibe ko rasiyā |

rāma lakhana sītā mana basiyā ‖ 8

Some folk teach their sons to emulate Ram the ideal man, others train their daughters to be the devoted wife like Sita, yet others groom themselves to be Laxman, the alert and readily available brother for the entire family.

Leap transcending the WATERS.
To meet Mother Sita, the Soul and Being of planet Earth.

# This leap into the unknown is called Faith.

This is possible because Hanuman has implicit Faith in his chosen Lord, Sri Ram.

Hanuman singing the glory of Lord Ram and Mother Sita

## 9 Seal of Humility

सूक्ष्म रूप धरि सियहिं दिखावा ।
बिकट रूप धरि लंक जरावा ॥ ९

sūkṣma rūpa dhari siyahiṃ dikhāvā |

bikaṭa rūpa dhari laṃka jarāvā || 9

The seal of the King is stamped with distinct humility and humble becomes man as he grows in wealth and status.

The formidable ego cannot face the loving humility, and gets charred to ashes in its presence, just as a high-tension filled concrete-city-dweller yearns for and finds succor in the pleasant welcoming glades and fresh pools of the out of the way small country side.

## 10 Raging Demons Quelled

भीम रूप धरि असुर सँहारे ।
रामचंद्र के काज सँवारे ॥ १०

bhīma rūpa dhari asura saṃhāre |

rāmacaṃdra ke kāja saṃvāre || 10

The raging demons in the mind fueled by anger hate vulgarity and intoxication, get vanquished effortlessly when the magnanimous magnificent glance of the great Lord strikes.

And this vision of the pleasing Lord Rama, whosoever is fortunate enough to partake of, knows his to-do list is well taken care of, and his tasks and targets get smoothly accomplished.

Leap transcending the LANDS.

To get the magic medicinal herb.

# This leap beyond the known is called Faith.

It is possible since Hanuman is well-grounded in his Master,
Lord Ram.

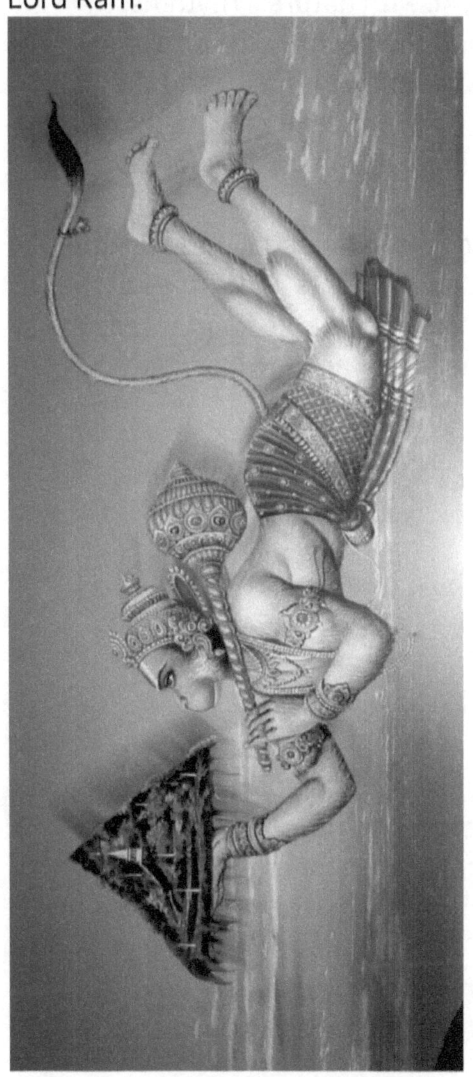

## 11 Sanjivani Magic Herb

लाय सजीवन लखन जियाये ।

श्रीरघुबीर हरषि उर लाये ॥ ११

lāya sajīvana lakhana jiyāye |

śrīraghubīra haraṣi ura lāye ॥ 11


When your mind gets in sync with nature's rhythms, then you see possibilities beyond the obvious, life's strong current then erupts like a beautiful fountain, and the committed get energized by your healing touch, thereby the term of the dedicated and honest man gets extended.

Family rejoices when term gets extended. Suddenly one begins to see the extraordinary talents and virtues of the same person whom we had begin to take for granted, and stopped appreciating, praising, or acknowledging.


## 12 Birth of Contentment

रघुपति कीन्ही बहुत बड़ाई ।

तुम मम प्रिय भरतहि सम भाई ॥ १२

raghupati kīnhī bahuta baḍaāī |

tuma mama priya bharatahi sama bhāī ॥ 12


The noble Lord rejoices with us, He too partakes of our joy, and that infuses in us a deep bonding, repairing frayed emotions, clearing away misunderstandings, and rediscovering our harmony and sense of togetherness.

Total contentment is born, fullness surfaces, even the deepest cracks and craters of the mind get filled and healed.

## 13 Shower of Grace

सहस बदन तुम्हरो जस गावैं ।
अस कहि श्रीपति कंठ लगावैं ॥ १३

sahasa badana tumharo jasa gāvaiṃ |

asa kahi śrīpati kaṃṭha lagāvaiṃ || 13

The one who causes such bonding and enables extension of lifespan or term of service, his physical being glows, radiates, and his aura spreads far and wide.

The good Lord showers love on his impeccable devotee, from whose heart gratefulness springs.


## 14 Witness by Noble Souls

सनकादिक ब्रह्मादि मुनीसा ।
नारद सारद सहित अहीसा ॥ १४

sanakādika brahmādi munīsā |

nārada sārada sahita ahīsā || 14

This spectacle is witnessed by many divine and noble souls, including the future seer Narada, one's ever alert wise companion Sesha, four exceptionally gifted 5-year old innocent child sages Sanaka etc., Lord Brahma and other Gods etc., who have planetEarth citizenship and who move freely due to their broad acceptability. Also the energy Saraswati sitting on the tongue of all Education.

Note: The four enlightened child sages are सनक Sanaka, सनन्दन Sanandan, सनातन Sanātan, सनत कुमार Sanat Kumar.

## 15 Cardinal Directions Hail

जम कुबेर दिगपाल जहाँ ते ।
कबि कोबिद कहि सकैं कहाँ ते ॥ १५

jama kubera digapāla jahām̐ te |
kabi kobida kahi sakaiṃ kahām̐ te ‖ 15

Yama, the self-preservation instinct;
Kubera, the wealth-generation desire;

Dikpala, guardians of the four cardinal directions, including
East for Brilliance & Anger,
South for Stability and Lust,
West for Family life and Frivolous behavior, and
North for Divinity and Arrogance;

Kavi-Kovid sake Director-Producer duo;

they all rejoice upon seeing the good Lord honor His
principal devotee.

Jakhoo Hanuman Temple, Shimla

## 16 Guarding the Village and Community

तुम उपकार सुग्रीवहिं कीन्हा ।

राम मिलाय राज पद दीन्हा ॥ १६

tuma upakāra sugrīvahiṃ kīnhā |

rāma milāya rāja pada dīnhā ॥ 16

By the honor thus gained, even your family-village-lineage, nay your property and possessions, all attain a divine status, all are guarded and protected by the Lord Himself.


## 17 Core Values Established

तुम्हरो मंत्र बिभीषन माना ।

लंकेस्वर भए सब जग जाना ॥ १७

tumharo maṃtra bibhīṣana mānā |

laṃkesvara bhae saba jaga jānā ॥ 17

Such a supreme self-effacing devotee influences even the die-hard opposing forces, and draws key men from there to join his company.

Thereby the values of Patience, Kindness, Forgiveness, Friendliness, Helpfulness and Belongingness, all get nourished and well-established in the nation.

Leap across SPACE.

## To meet the Sun, who powers all beings.

This leap is a dive into the vastness, into infinity.

It is impossible without Faith in one's Guru, Lord Sri Ram.

54 feet high Hanuman with mace, Sarangpur Temple, Gujarat

## 18 Mighty Sun Visits

जुग सहस्त्र जोजन पर भानु ।

लील्यो ताहि मधुर फल जानू ॥ १८

juga sahastra jojana para bhānu |

līlyo tāhi madhura phala jānū || 18

Seeing this luster and glow in your city, even the mighty Sun pays a respectful congratulatory visit to your nation, leaping through the vast intervening distance by space-warp, and also masking his own fiery red brilliance during the corresponding timespan.

## 19 Trusted Emissary

प्रभु मुद्रिका मेलि मुख माहीं ।

जलधि लाँघि गये अचरज नाहीं ॥ १९

prabhu mudrikā meli mukha māhīṃ |

jaladhi lāṁghi gaye acaraja nāhīṃ || 19

Thee are the messenger for feedback and affirmatory seal of Lord's darshan. Your purity level has reached the stage whereby your gesture becomes the confirmation that one has truly experienced the blessings of the Lord and that the vision one saw is the great Lord's, and not any hearsay.

Even for the fair maidens at home, you alone act as the postman that carries the messages from their far-faring beloved husbands.
You alone are the trusted emissary responsible for delivering precious diamonds and confidential documents between nations at treaty or wealthy businessmen exploring new markets.

Your facial expression is unmistakable - none can imitate, your gait is typical - hard to emulate, your body's footprint is infinitesimal - you can enter even the impregnable and maximum-security guarded fortresses.

## 20 Infallible Ambassador

दुर्गम काज जगत के जेते ।

सुगम अनुग्रह तुम्हरे तेते ॥ २०

durgama kāja jagata ke jete |

sugama anugraha tumhare tete || 20

So it is no surprise that the top men hire you alone, the best nations regard you as their infallible ambassador for top-secret pacts, for the wealthiest there is no alternative when it comes to hard negotiations, and the fair maiden chooses you alone for contacting her beloved.

All divisive, arrogant, tumultuous, and hard to satisfy forces lose their zeal in your presence, mother Earth's innocent children's tasks get easily done.

## 21 Cultivation of Gratefulness

राम दुआरे तुम रखवारे ।

होत न आज्ञा बिनु पैसारे ॥ २१

rāma duāre tuma rakhavāre |

hota na ājñā binu paisāre || 21

Gratefulness. Gratitude in day to day life. Feeling loved by the Lord. Irrespective of whether the situation is troublesome, the person is demanding, or the weather is unforgiving, when one's heart has accepted the Lord's will, then one's attitude becomes graceful, come what may.

And this attitude is rare, such temperament is hard to find.

A few years are needed to cultivate such grace, to nurture and instill such values in the heart. When that time-period is up, when one graduates so as to say, then the MAGIC begins.

## 22 Befriends the Forces of Nature

सब सुख लहै तुम्हारी सरना ।

तुम रच्छक काहू को डरना ॥ २२

saba sukha lahai tumhārī saranā |

tuma racchaka kāhū ko ḍaranā || 22

Then all the forces of Nature become friendly, protective, caring. Then every man and institution become favorable. Time and Space have played their hand, and you are now qualified for the Ultimate sojourn.

LIFE is precious, this understanding dawns. From that moment, your speech, actions, emotions get elevated, and the Divine gates open for you.

Once the Divine envelops you, life becomes a charm. It twinkles like the stars. Your smile becomes the passport. Your ambitions get satiated, all targets are exceeded.

## 23 Glow Radiates Far and Wide

आपन तेज सम्हारो आपै ।

तीनों लोक हाँक तें काँपै ॥ २३

āpana teja samhāro āpai |

tīnoṃ loka hāṃka teṃ kāṃpai ॥ 23

Your brilliance cannot be contained. Your glow radiates throughout the globe. All sense your magnificent, excellent, overpowering presence.

But natural all bow down and seek your protection.

## 24 Contains the Terrible Energies

भूत पिसाच निकट नहिं आवै ।

महाबीर जब नाम सुनावै ॥ २४

bhūta pisāca nikaṭa nahiṃ āvai |

mahābīra jaba nāma sunāvai ॥ 24

Even the reptiles and scorpions assure the noble ones of their non-interference, hence safety. Even the devastating forces of lust and greed remain far away from your city and denizens.

Your name Mahavir - the resolute chivalrous brave - is stamped on the hearts of cheering happy folk.

## 25 Embodiment of Strength

नासै रोग हरै सब पीरा ।

जपत निरंतर हनुमत बीरा ॥ २५

nāsai roga harai saba pīrā |

japata niraṃtara hanumata bīrā || 25

O embodiment of Strength! Your name Hanuman and emotion related to your superhuman deeds is enough to infuse valor and willpower and burn all toxins, thus curing diseases and eradicating pain of all sorts

21$^{st}$ June 2020

## 26 Merits of Chanting Chalisa

संकट तें हनुमान छुड़ावै ।

मन क्रम बचन ध्यान जो लावै ॥ २६

saṃkaṭa teṃ hanumāna chuḍāvai |

mana krama bacana dhyāna jo lāvai || 26

In fact it has been repeatedly proven that chanting the Hanuman Chalisa with innocence, intensity and purity of devotion is a veritable panacea to banish fear of any kind. These verses and couplets produce a sound shield that remains in effect for a sufficiently long period of time.

Hanuman the mighty warrior surrenders effortlessly at the feet of Lord Ram. He is the perfect devotee.

# Q. What is the meaning of Guru?

He is the path, the vision, the protection, and the absolute aim.

# Q. Who is Lord Sri Ram?

He is the glow, the effulgence, the purity, the divinity that each one of us yearns for in the deepest cave of one's heart.

# Q. Is Guru and God the same?

One's Guru shall surely guide us to the Lord, to the Source, to the Ultimate Bliss.

# Q. Who is a Devotee?

A devotee is the one who has implicit Faith. Who has impeccable Devotion. Who is humble, supple, grateful and ready to serve.

# Q. Is Guru and Devotee the same?

Guru manifests through his devotee, just as the Lord manifests through the Guru.

## 27 Lord Ram and the Perfect Devotee

सब पर राम तपस्वी राजा ।

तिनके काज सकल तुम साजा ॥ २७

saba para rāma tapasvī rājā |

tinake kāja sakala tuma sājā ‖ 27


The great Lord Ram was a true and total benefactor of the populace, and it was thee who obediently and cheerfully carried out His dictums. You are hailed as the perfect devotee.


## 28 Responsibility Eulogized

और मनोरथ जो कोई लावै ।

सोई अमित जीवन फल पावै ॥ २८

aura manoratha jo koī lāvai |

soī amita jīvana phala pāvai ‖ 28


Similarly,
    if anyone serves society cheerfully and caringly,
    shoulders responsibility of his family properly, and
    does his duty respectfully,
earns your everlasting grace and protection.

## 29 Legendary Exploits

चारों जुग परताप तुम्हारा ।
है परसिद्ध जगत उजियारा ॥ २९

cāroṃ juga paratāpa tumhārā |

hai parasiddha jagata ujiyārā || 29

You have become a legend for all to emulate through the ages. Your exploits fill the hearts of children with glee. Far and wide is your glory sung, the entire planet resounds with innumerable tales of your scintillating deeds recounted at firesides.

Hanuman Temple, Arsha Vidya Gurukulam, Dorli, Nagpur

## 30 Saintly vs the Cruel

साधु संत के तुम रखवारे ।

असुर निकंदन राम दुलारे ॥ ३०

sādhu saṃta ke tuma rakhavāre |

asura nikaṃdana rāma dulāre || 30

Of the kind-hearted hard-working honest men you are their immaculate shield.

The cruel and lazy and dishonest tremble when your name is chanted, and forget their troublesome ways.

You are the favorite of the great Lord Ram, whose purifying presence is distinctly experienced in your amazing company.


## 31 Eight Siddhi Nine Nidhi

अष्ट सिद्धि नौ निधि के दाता ।

अस बर दीन्ह जानकी माता ॥ ३१

aṣṭa siddhi nau nidhi ke dātā |

asa bara dīnha jānakī mātā || 31

There are 8 types of Siddhi. These are skills attained after lot of tapas by various seekers, disciples, yogis and brilliant hard-working individuals. These Siddhis are named:

1. Animā Siddhi – by which matter can be reduced to an atom without losing any characteristics
2. Mahimā Siddhi – by which matter can be enlarged to the size of the planet, retaining its qualities
3. Garimā Siddhi – becoming solid and immovable due to enormous weight

4. Laghimā Siddhi – becoming light as a feather so that the softest breeze can carry away
5. Prāpti Siddhi – able to travel the extent of creation
6. Prākāmya Siddhi – desires get fulfilled before they arise
7. Ishitva Siddhi – dominion over all men and nature
8. Vashitva Siddhi – capacity to win any debate, battle, or spiritual realm

Also there are 9 types of Nidhi. These are wealths attained after lot of tapas by various seekers, disciples, yogis and brilliant hard-working individuals. These Nidhis are named:
1. VIVEKA intellectual certainty
2. VAIRĀGYA emotional certainty
3. SHAMA Peaceful Intellect
4. DAMA Balanced Senses
5. TITIKSHĀ having the guts and stamina to tide over troublesome and challenging situations and persons.
6. UPARATI having the foresight to enjoy all granted pleasures and be grateful for even the tiniest boons.
7. SHRADDHĀ working hard on strengthening your faith in the goodness of creation, in the nobleness of mankind, and in the grace of time and tide.
8. Samadhan equitable countenance, satisfied lifestyle.
9. MUMUKSHATVA desire to be free and rise above the mundane

*For the materialistic-minded, there is a couplet giving the 9 wealths as:*

महापद्मश्च पद्मश्च शंखो मकर कच्छपौ ।

मुकुंदकुंद नीलाश्च सर्वश्च निधयो नव ॥

O Hanuman! You are the ultimate since you have attained all the 8 Siddhi and all the 9 Nidhi, by the grace of Supreme Mother Sita.

Furthermore, by the collective consciousness of planet earth, named Janaki, you have been empowered to grant one or more of these great Siddhi Nidhi, to deserving individuals who seek your devotion and protection.

## 32 Chemical Formulae of the Alchemist

राम रसायन तुम्हरे पासा ।

सदा रहो रघुपति के दासा ॥ ३२

rāma rasāyana tumhare pāsā |

sadā raho raghupati ke dāsā || 32

O Hanuman! You have the chemical formulae that are much sought for by alchemists, scientists, innovators, developers and inventors.

Please keep on doing the good work, keep on inspiring us and our children, and be with us till the end O Hanuman!

## 33 Lifetimes Purified by Thee

तुम्हरे भजन राम को पावै ।

जनम जनम के दुख बिसरावै ॥ ३३

tumhare bhajana rāma ko pāvai |

janama janama ke dukha bisarāvai || 33

Singing your glories we too attain to the Divine Grace of Lord Ram. We too are accepted as our faith becomes deep, our heart becomes cleansed and free of fear.

## 34 Man Machine Nature Supports till End

अंत काल रघुबर पुर जाई ।

जहाँ जन्म हरिभक्त कहाई ॥ ३४

amta kāla raghubara pura jāī |

jahāṁ janma haribhakta kahāī || 34

You are so devoted to the Ultimate Consciousness Brahman, that nature, man, machine, and the entire creation loves you and professes belongingness towards you.

Your presence amongst us instills devotion to Lord Hari, and your presence lasts eternally within us.

## 35 Exemplary Traits Core Definition

और देवता चित्त न धरई ।

हनुमत सेइ सर्ब सुख करई ॥ ३५

aura devatā citta na dharaī |

hanumata sei sarba sukha karaī || 35

Many gods and goddesses are there in creation.

In the numerous cultures, races, states and kingdoms scattered over the planet, different men pray to different deities. Various beings worship various values, some talents and qualities are respected more, and a multitude of famous and legendary men and women have hence emerged.

One quality that is undoubtedly coveted and worshipped by one and all is superhuman Strength. Total lack of Fear. Exemplary Courage. Instant YES Attitude and Service oriented Mindset.

This is what sums you O Hanuman! This is your core definition. This is the template you have given to the world.

These are the basic virtues that define our movie heroes and heroines. These are the skills stamped on the pages of comics filled with attractive damsels and heroic males, and these are the talents that earn the maximum; whether in the arena of Business, Sports, or Entertainment.

## 36 Nurture the Physical Mental Emotional

संकट कटै मिटै सब पीरा ।

जो सुमिरै हनुमत बलबीरा ॥ ३६

saṃkaṭa kaṭai miṭai saba pīrā |

jo sumirai hanumata balabīrā ॥ 36

Whosoever nurtures the values of physical fitness, mental alertness, emotional purity, and spiritual calmness, they get to move forward in life. They get to attain unprecedented success. They tower over their brothers and sisters; they leave their mark in this world.

They capture the imagination of mankind. They become the stuff of legends. They are what parents hope their children shall emulate, they are whom saints recount in dialogs with their disciples.

O Man! Seek ways to get aligned with such traits. Seek schools where these are taught, seek jobs where these are appreciated, and live in neighborhoods where these abound.

Physical Fitness.
Mental Alertness.
Emotional Purity.
Spiritual Calmness.
Belongingness and Sharing.

## 37 Victory to You and to Yours

जै जै जै हनुमान गोसाईं ।

कृपा करहु गुरुदेव की नाईं ॥ ३७

jai jai jai hanumāna gosāīṃ |

kṛpā karahu gurudeva kī nāīṃ ॥ 37

Victory Victory Victory to these Values. May ye prosper, may ye be sought for, may ye be empowered by the enlightened Masters. May we all likewise seek and find the Guru; may we align to the tradition of the sacrosanct teachings.

## 38 Sing 100 Times in 100 Days

जो सत बार पाठ कर कोई ।

छूटहि बंदि महा सुख होई ॥ ३८

jo sata bāra pāṭha kara koī |

chūṭahi baṃdi mahā sukha hoī ॥ 38

Whosoever a 100 times over a hundred days (3 months or a quarter year, with little extra to account for exigencies), strives to imbibe these traits,
    Shall be blessed for life with them.
    Shall have these values etched in their brain and firmly established in their heart.
    Shall always be protected against grave danger and impassable storms.
    Shall be taken care of by the Divine,

so it has been boldly stated.

## 39 The Takeaway of Chanting

जो यह पढ़ै हनुमान चालीसा ।
होय सिद्धि साखी गौरीसा ॥ ३९

jo yaha paḍhaai hanumāna cālīsā |

hoya siddhi sākhī gaurīsā || 39

Again it is so reiterated.
Nurture  and ingrain the values stated:
      KSHAMĀ Forgiveness
      DAYĀ Compassion
      ĀRJAVAM Sincerity
      SATYAM Truth
      SAMĀDHĀN Contentment.
*(from the Ashtavakra Gita - virtues to overcome misery).*

Be focused in attainment of the wealths:
Viveka intellectual certainty
Vairāgya emotional certainty
Shama Peaceful Intellect
Dama Balanced Senses
Titikshā having the guts and stamina to tide over
      troublesome and challenging situations and persons.
Uparati having the foresight to enjoy all granted pleasures
      and be grateful for even the tiniest boons.
Shraddhā working hard on strengthening your faith in the
      goodness of creation, in the nobleness of mankind,
      and in the grace of time and tide.
Samādhān equitable countenance, satisfied lifestyle.
Mumukshatva desire to be free and rise above the opposites,

rise above pleasure and pain, and seek the ultimate - the
one beyond reason, experience, history.
*(from the Viveka Chudamani of Adi Sankara - qualifications
for a seeker of Brahman).*

Shama **self-control and quietness of mind.**
Vichāra (Viveka) **spirit of enquiry for the truth.**
Santosha **emotional contentment in everyday life.**
Satsanga **company of the wise, company of devotees,
        discipleship of a saint.**
*(from Yoga Vasistha – 4 gatekeepers to the realm of freedom)*

Yama **personal discipline,** Niyama **society protocols,** Asana
**pleasing exercise,** Pranayama **breath control,** Pratyahara
**tendency to go inwards,** and Dharana Dhyana Samadhi =
Sanyam **Contemplation Meditation Union.**
*(from Patanjali Yoga Sutras – the 8 limbs of Yoga or Divine
Union).*

## 40 The Author Submits

तुलसीदास सदा हरि चेरा ।
कीजै नाथ हृदय महँ डेरा ॥ ४०

tulasīdāsa sadā hari cerā |

kījai nātha hṛdaya mahaṁ ḍerā ॥ 40

The writer of this sacrosanct text, Tulsidas, now pens his
name, and fondly hopes that the Lord shall consider him a
dear devotee.

Tulsidas also prays for the good Lord to be benevolent
towards him in the future, and that his family,
neighborhood, state and planet shall be visited again and

again by the Lord, shall be given guidance and protection in times to come through ways and means that are relevant and contemporary.

Hanuman Idol at Mahabir Dal Temple, Bathinda, consecrated on 12th February 2007.

# Epilogue

‖ दोहा ‖ dohā ‖ Quatrain

पवनतनय संकट हरन

    मंगल मूरति रूप ।

राम लखन सीता सहित

    हृदय बसहु सुर भूप ‖

pavanatanaya saṃkaṭa harana

    maṃgala mūrati rūpa |

rāma lakhana sītā sahita

    hṛdaya basahu sura bhūpa ‖

O Breath physical! O Prana subtle! O Life sustainer! O
Obstacle vanquisher! O Radiant one! O Handsome Hero!

May my heart reach out to thee in devotion.
May my reason accept my planet and its ways with elan.
May my soul attain its target of purity divinity
enlightenment.

---

Jai Gurudev 4:16pm 23.9.2023 Patiala Home.

Hanuman with Ram and Laxman Painting

46

# Hanuman and the Legends

Hanuman figures prominently in both the Indian epics, viz, the Ramayan and the Mahabharat.


## Hanuman and Arjun

Hanuman serves as the Flag-bearer on the chariot of Arjun, with Lord Krishna as the charioteer, and thus protects the chariot from any scratch.


## Hanuman and Bhim

Hanuman's alert intervention breaks his younger brother Bhim's ego, and empowers Bhim with extraordinary strength.


## Hanuman and Lord Shiva

Hanuman pleases Lord Shiva with his mighty prowess, and obtains the boon of immortality.


## Hanuman and the Sun

Hanuman ingrains wisdom from the Sun, and as his foremost student, brings the delightful glow of the Sun to planet Earth.


## Hanuman and Sugreev

Hanuman serves as the chief general of King Sugreev, and helps him in many victories and thereby keep his kingdom intact.


## Hanuman and Vibhishan

Hanuman guides Vibhishan, the brother of Ravan, to the path of righteousness.


## Hanuman and Sita

Hanuman brings the seal of Lord Ram to Mother Sita in Lanka, and attains from her the 8 Siddhi and 9 Nidhi.


## Hanuman and Laxman

Hanuman's timely delivery of the medicinal herb Sanjivani, revives the unconscious Laxman.

# Hanuman's Birthplace

Hanuman Temple board giving details that Hanuman was born here in Kishkindha hills at Hampi, Karnataka

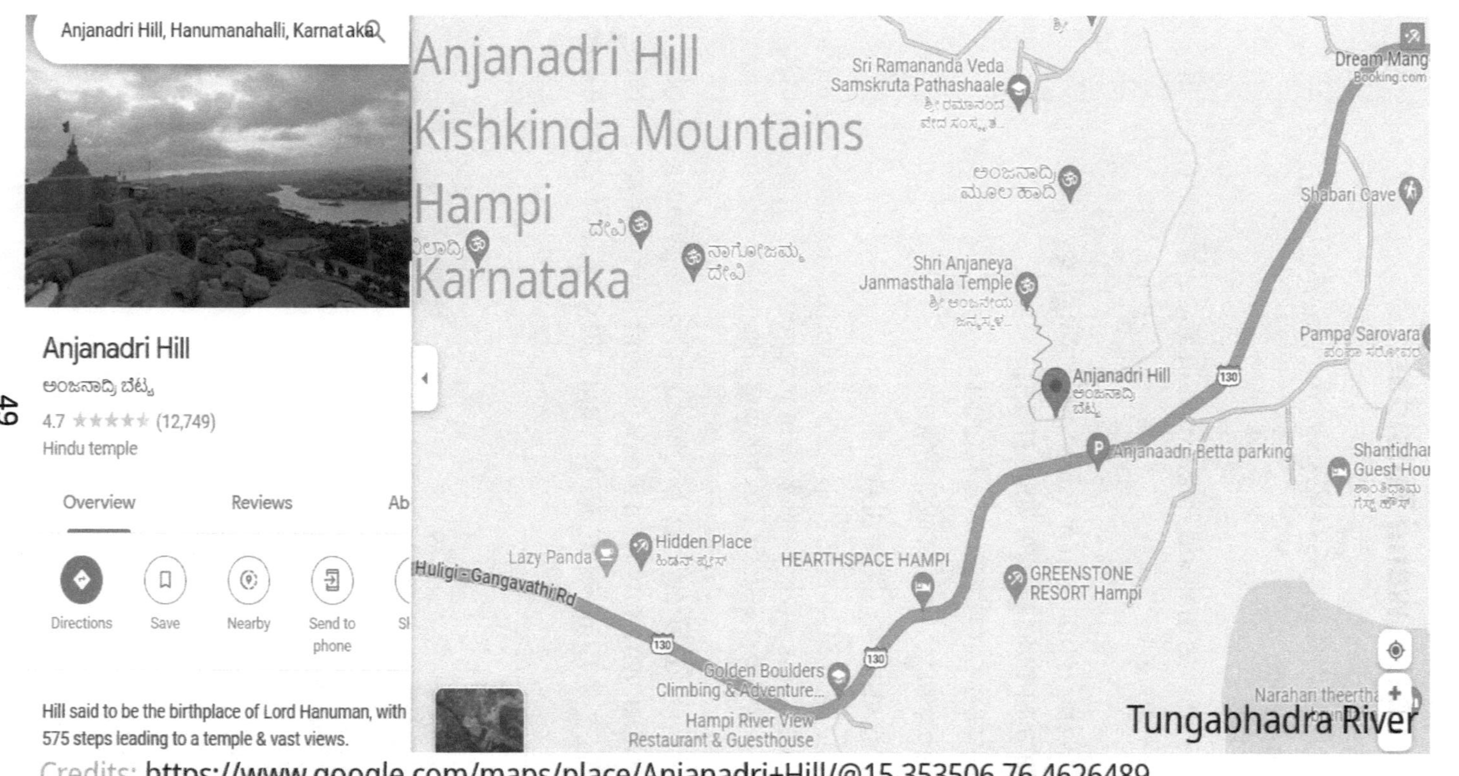


Credits: https://www.google.com/maps/place/Anjanadri+Hill/@15.353506,76.4626489

49

## About Goswami Tulsidas

Tulsidas is revered as the Sage Valmiki reborn in the 16th century CE.

Tulsidas was married to Ratnavali, and was extremely in love with her.

Once she rebuked him with these stinging words:

लाज न लागत आपुको दौरे आयहु साथ ।

धिक धिक ऐसे प्रेमको कहा कहहु मैं नाथ ॥

अस्थिचर्ममय देह मम तामें जैसी प्रीति ।

तैसी जो श्रीराम महँ होत न तौ भवभीति ॥

If only thee would develop such passionate devotion to Lord Sri Ram, (as your loving attachment towards myself), you would leap through the storms of life and attain final beatitude.

This episode proved to be the turning point in the life of Tulsidas, who took to a life of fervent devotion towards the Lord, and attained Enlightenment so coveted by noble men.

Goswami Tulsidas, from a contemporary Painting

# Latin Transliteration Chart

International Alphabet of Sanskrit Transliteration (I.A.S.T.)

| a | अ | ā | आ | i | इ | ī | ई | u | उ | ū | ऊ | ṛ | ऋ | ṝ | ॠ | ḷ | ऌ | | |
|---|---|---|---|---|---|---|---|---|---|---|---|---|---|---|---|---|---|---|---|
| | | | | | | | | | | | | ◌ৄ | | ◌ৄ | | ◌ৄ | | | |
| e | ए | ai | ऐ | o | ओ | au | औ | ṃ | ◌ं | m̐ | ◌ँ | ḥ | ◌: | Ardha Visarga | ◌꙯ | oṃ | ॐ | | |

Consonants shown with vowel 'a= अ' for uttering

| ka | क | ca | च | ṭa | ट | ta | त | pa | प |
|---|---|---|---|---|---|---|---|---|---|
| kha | ख | cha | छ | ṭha | ठ | tha | थ | pha | फ |
| ga | ग | ja | ज | ḍa | ड | da | द | ba | ब |
| gha | घ | jha | झ | ḍha | ढ | dha | ध | bha | भ |
| ṅa | ङ | ña | ञ | ṇa | ण | na | न | ma | म |

| ya | ra | la | va | | ḷa | ' | |
|---|---|---|---|---|---|---|---|
| य | र | ल | व | | ळ | S | |
| | | | | | Consonant only | | |
| śa | ṣa | sa | ha | | ka | क्अ = क | |
| श | ष | स | ह | | k | क् | |

# Verses for Chanting

श्री हनूमते नमः ॥ ॐ हं हनूमते नमः ॥

## ॥ श्री हनुमान चालीसा ॥

॥ दोहा ॥

श्रीगुरु चरन सरोज रज
        निज मनु मुकुरु सुधारि ।
बरनउँ रघुबर बिमल जसु
        जो दायकु फल चारि ॥

बुद्धिहीन तनु जानिके
        सुमिरौं पवनकुमार ।
बल बुधि बिद्या देहु मोहिं
        हरहु कलेस बिकार ॥

॥ चौपाई ॥

जय हनुमान ज्ञान गुण सागर ।
जय कपीस तिहुँ लोक उजागर ॥ १

राम दूत अतुलित बल धामा ।
अंजनिपुत्र पवनसुत नामा ॥ २

महाबीर बिक्रम बजरंगी ।
कुमति निवार सुमति के संगी ॥ ३

कंचन बरन बिराज सुबेसा ।
कानन कुंडल कुंचित केसा ॥ ४

हाथ बज्र औ ध्वजा बिराजै ।
काँधे मूँज जनेऊ साजै ॥ ५

संकर सुवन केसरी नंदन ।
तेज प्रताप महा जग बंदन ॥ ६

बिद्यावान गुणी अति चातुर ।
राम काज करिबे को आतुर ॥ ७

प्रभु चरित्र सुनिबे को रसिया ।
राम लखन सीता मन बसिया ॥ ८

सूक्ष्म रूप धरि सियहिं दिखावा ।
बिकट रूप धरि लंक जरावा ॥ ९

भीम रूप धरि असुर सँहारे ।
रामचंद्र के काज सँवारे ॥ १०

लाय सजीवन लखन जियाये ।
श्रीरघुबीर हरषि उर लाये ॥ ११

रघुपति कीन्ही बहुत बड़ाई ।
तुम मम प्रिय भरतहि सम भाई ॥ १२

सहस बदन तुम्हरो जस गावैं ।
अस कहि श्रीपति कंठ लगावैं ॥ १३

सनकादिक ब्रह्मादि मुनीसा ।
नारद सारद सहित अहीसा ॥ १४

जम कुबेर दिगपाल जहाँ ते ।
कबि कोबिद कहि सकैं कहाँ ते ॥ १५

तुम उपकार सुग्रीवहिं कीन्हा ।
राम मिलाय राज पद दीन्हा ॥ १६

तुम्हरो मंत्र बिभीषन माना ।
लंकेस्वर भए सब जग जाना ॥ १७

जुग सहस्र जोजन पर भानु ।
लील्यो ताहि मधुर फल जानू ॥ १८

प्रभु मुद्रिका मेलि मुख माहीं ।
जलधि लाँघि गये अचरज नाहीं ॥ १९

दुर्गम काज जगत के जेते ।
सुगम अनुग्रह तुम्हरे तेते ॥ २०

राम दुआरे तुम रखवारे ।
होत न आज्ञा बिनु पैसारे ॥ २१

सब सुख लहै तुम्हारी सरना ।
तुम रच्छक काहू को डरना ॥ २२

आपन तेज सम्हारो आपै ।
तीनों लोक हाँक तें काँपै ॥ २३

भूत पिसाच निकट नहिं आवै ।
महाबीर जब नाम सुनावै ॥ २४

नासै रोग हरै सब पीरा ।
जपत निरंतर हनुमत बीरा ॥ २५

संकट तें हनुमान छुड़ावै ।
मन क्रम बचन ध्यान जो लावै ॥ २६

सब पर राम तपस्वी राजा ।
तिनके काज सकल तुम साजा ॥ २७

और मनोरथ जो कोई लावै ।
सोई अमित जीवन फल पावै ॥ २८

चारों जुग परताप तुम्हारा ।
है परसिद्ध जगत उजियारा ॥ २९

साधु संत के तुम रखवारे ।
असुर निकंदन राम दुलारे ॥ ३०

अष्ट सिद्धि नौ निधि के दाता ।
अस बर दीन्ह जानकी माता ॥ ३१

राम रसायन तुम्हरे पासा ।
सदा रहो रघुपति के दासा ॥ ३२

तुम्हरे भजन राम को पावै ।
जनम जनम के दुख बिसरावै ॥ ३३

अंत काल रघुबर पुर जाई ।
जहाँ जन्म हरिभक्त कहाई ॥ ३४

और देवता चित्त न धरई ।
हनुमत सेइ सर्ब सुख करई ॥ ३५

संकट कटै मिटै सब पीरा ।
जो सुमिरै हनुमत बलबीरा ॥ ३६

जै जै जै हनुमान गोसाईं ।
कृपा करहु गुरुदेव की नाई ॥ ३७

जो सत बार पाठ कर कोई ।
छूटहि बंदि महा सुख होई ॥ ३८

जो यह पढ़ै हनुमान चालीसा ।
होय सिद्धि साखी गौरीसा ॥ ३९

तुलसीदास सदा हरि चेरा ।
कीजै नाथ हृदय महँ डेरा ॥ ४०

॥ दोहा ॥
पवनतनय संकट हरन
       मंगल मूरति रूप ।
राम लखन सीता सहित
       हृदय बसहु सुर भूप ॥

--- ∞ ∞ ∞ ---

सियावर राम जय जय राम ।
मेरे प्रभु राम जय जय राम ॥

Hanuman black granite idol from Tamil Nadu

## || śrī hanumāna cālīsā ||

|| dohā ||

śrīguru carana saroja raja
　　　nija manu mukuru sudhāri |
baranauṁ raghubara bimala jasu
　　　jo dāyaku phala cāri ||

buddhihīna tanu jānike
　　　sumirauṃ pavanakumāra |
bala budhi bidyā dehu mohiṃ
　　　harahu kalesa bikāra ||

|| caupāī ||

jaya hanumāna jñāna guṇa sāgara |

jaya kapīsa tihuṁ loka ujāgara || 1

rāma dūta atulita bala dhāmā |

aṃjaniputra pavanasuta nāmā || 2

mahābīra bikrama bajaraṃgī |

kumati nivāra sumati ke saṃgī || 3

kaṃcana barana birāja subesā |

kānana kuṃḍala kuṃcita kesā || 4

hātha bajra au dhvajā birājai |

kāṁdhe mūṁja janeū sājai || 5

saṃkara suvana kesarī naṃdana |
teja pratāpa mahā jaga baṃdana || 6

bidyāvāna guṇī ati cātura |
rāma kāja karibe ko ātura || 7

prabhu caritra sunibe ko rasiyā |
rāma lakhana sītā mana basiyā || 8

sūkṣma rūpa dhari siyahiṃ dikhāvā |
bikaṭa rūpa dhari laṃka jarāvā || 9

bhīma rūpa dhari asura saṃhāre |
rāmacaṃdra ke kāja saṃvāre || 10

lāya sajīvana lakhana jiyāye |
śrīraghubīra haraṣi ura lāye || 11

raghupati kīnhī bahuta baḍaāī |
tuma mama priya bharatahi sama bhāī || 12

sahasa badana tumharo jasa gāvaiṃ |
asa kahi śrīpati kaṃṭha lagāvaiṃ || 13

sanakādika brahmādi munīsā |
nārada sārada sahita ahīsā || 14

jama kubera digapāla jahāṃ te |
kabi kobida kahi sakaiṃ kahāṃ te || 15

tuma upakāra sugrīvahiṃ kīnhā |
rāma milāya rāja pada dīnhā || 16

tumharo maṃtra bibhīṣana mānā |
laṃkesvara bhae saba jaga jānā || 17

juga sahastra jojana para bhānu |
līlyo tāhi madhura phala jānū || 18

prabhu mudrikā meli mukha māhīṃ |
jaladhi lāṁghi gaye acaraja nāhīṃ || 19

durgama kāja jagata ke jete |
sugama anugraha tumhare tete || 20

rāma duāre tuma rakhavāre |
hota na ājñā binu paisāre || 21

saba sukha lahai tumhārī saranā |
tuma racchaka kāhū ko ḍaranā || 22

āpana teja samhāro āpai |
tīnoṃ loka hāṁka teṃ kāṁpai || 23

bhūta pisāca nikaṭa nahiṃ āvai |
mahābīra jaba nāma sunāvai || 24

nāsai roga harai saba pīrā |
japata niraṃtara hanumata bīrā || 25

saṃkaṭa teṃ hanumāna chuḍāvai |
mana krama bacana dhyāna jo lāvai || 26

saba para rāma tapasvī rājā |
tinake kāja sakala tuma sājā || 27

aura manoratha jo koī lāvai |
soī amita jīvana phala pāvai || 28

cāroṃ juga paratāpa tumhārā |
hai parasiddha jagata ujiyārā || 29

sādhu saṃta ke tuma rakhavāre |
asura nikaṃdana rāma dulāre || 30

aṣṭa siddhi nau nidhi ke dātā |
asa bara dīnha jānakī mātā || 31

rāma rasāyana tumhare pāsā |
sadā raho raghupati ke dāsā || 32

tumhare bhajana rāma ko pāvai |
janama janama ke dukha bisarāvai || 33

aṃta kāla raghubara pura jāī |
jahāṃ janma haribhakta kahāī || 34

aura devatā citta na dharaī |
hanumata sei sarba sukha karaī || 35

saṃkaṭa kaṭai miṭai saba pīrā |

jo sumirai hanumata balabīrā || 36

jai jai jai hanumāna gosāīṃ |

kṛpā karahu gurudeva kī nāīṃ || 37

jo sata bāra pāṭha kara koī |

chūṭahi baṃdi mahā sukha hoī || 38

jo yaha paḍhaai hanumāna cālīsā |

hoya siddhi sākhī gaurīsā || 39

tulasīdāsa sadā hari cerā |

kījai nātha hṛdaya mahaṁ ḍerā || 40

|| dohā ||
pavanatanaya saṃkaṭa harana

    maṃgala mūrati rūpa |
rāma lakhana sītā sahita

    hṛdaya basahu sura bhūpa ||


--- ∞ ∞ ∞ ---

siyāvara rāma jaya jaya rāma |
mere prabhu rāma jaya jaya rāma ||

# Sanskrit Grammar

Sandhis separated word by word पदच्छेद (प॰),
and with विभक्ति Cases have been listed.


<u>Abbreviations</u>
Nouns
> **m** masculine, **f** feminine, **n** neuter; **V** vocative
> **1/1** = vibhakti from 1 to 7/number 1 to 3
> adj = adjective, adv = adverb


Indeclinables (uninflected nouns or verbs) **0.**
In Sanskrit the **adverbs** are mostly uninflected.
Adjective follows a Substantive in case and number.


Verbs
> **iii/1** = person i to iii / number 1 to 3
> **PPP** = Past Participle Passive = क्त
> **PPA** = Past Participle Active = क्तवत्
> **PrPA** = Present Participle Active = शतृ / शानच्
> **FPA** = Future Participle Active = लृट् + शतृ
> **PoPP** = Potential Participle Passive = य, तव्य, अनीयर्
> (gerundive)


It is a common practice in Sanskrit grammar to use a
"hyphen" to indicate compounds.
Compound or समास is frequently encountered in Sanskrit
literature. It has a beauty and a brevity.

Since Sanskrit is an inflectional language, the **spelling of the same word** changes as per context or usage. Hence words can be **placed anywhere** in a sentence, as in poetic use, without change in meaning. The matrix shows how.

**Verb inflections in Sanskrit – a sample chart**

| 982 गम्ॢ गतौ – to go, also in the sense of attainment | | | |
| --- | --- | --- | --- |
| Present Tense Active voice लट् कर्त्तरि | | | |
| Person/no | singular | dual | plural |
| Third | गच्छति iii/1 | गच्छतः iii/2 | गच्छन्ति iii/3 |
| Second | गच्छसि ii/1 | गच्छथः ii/2 | गच्छथ ii/3 |
| First | गच्छामि i/1 | गच्छावः i/2 | गच्छामः i/3 |

**Noun declensions in Sanskrit – a sample chart**

| Masculine stem, vowel अ ending | | | |
| --- | --- | --- | --- |
| (र्–आ–म्–अ) राम m Lord's name | | | |
| | singular [1] | dual [2] | plural [3] |
| 1 Doer | रामः 1/1 | रामौ 1/2 | रामाः 1/3 |
| 2 Object | रामम् 2/1 | रामौ 2/2 | रामान् 2/3 |
| 3 by | रामेण 3/1 | रामाभ्याम् 3/2 | रामैः 3/3 |
| 4 for | रामाय 4/1 | रामाभ्याम् 4/2 | रामेभ्यः 4/3 |
| 5 from | रामात् 5/1 | रामाभ्याम् 5/2 | रामेभ्यः 5/3 |
| 6 of | रामस्य 6/1 | रामयोः 6/2 | रामाणाम् 6/3 |
| 7 in | रामे 7/1 | रामयोः 7/2 | रामेषु 7/3 |
| Vocative | हे राम V/1 | हे रामौ V/2 | हे रामाः V/3 |

## Masculine stem, consonant त् ending

| मरुत् [m] Wind, Breeze, Air | | | |
|---|---|---|---|
| | singular [1] | dual [2] | plural [3] |
| 1 Doer | मरुत् [1/1] | मरुतौ [1/2] | मरुतः [1/3] |
| 2 Object | मरुतम् [2/1] | मरुतौ [2/2] | मरुतः [2/3] |
| 3 by | मरुता [3/1] | मरुद्भ्याम् [3/2] | मरुद्भिः [3/3] |
| 4 for | मरुते [4/1] | मरुद्भ्याम् [4/2] | मरुद्भ्यः [4/3] |
| 5 from | मरुतः [5/1] | मरुद्भ्याम् [5/2] | मरुद्भ्यः [5/3] |
| 6 of | मरुतः [6/1] | मरुतोः [6/2] | मरुताम् [6/3] |
| 7 in | मरुति [7/1] | मरुतोः [7/2] | मरुत्सु [7/3] |
| Vocative | हे मरुत् [V/1] | हे मरुतौ [V/2] | हे मरुतः [V/3] |

## Moods and Tenses in Sanskrit

| 1 | लट् | Present Tense |
|---|---|---|
| 2 | लुङ् | Aorist Past Tense, before from now |
| 3 | लङ् | Imperfect Past Tense – before from yesterday onwards |
| 4 | लिट् | Perfect Past Tense – distant unseen past |
| 5 | लृट् | Simple Future Tense – now onwards |
| 6 | लुट् | Periphrastic Future Tense – tomorrow onwards |
| 7 | लृङ् | Conditional Mood - if/then, past or future |
| 8 | लोट् | Imperative Mood – request |
| 9 | विधि० | Potential Mood – order विधिलिङ् |
| 10 | आशिर् | Benedictive Mood – blessing आशीर्लिङ् (also used in the sense of a curse) |

# Conjugation process of Verb

अधीते <sup>लट् iii/1</sup> = she/he learns with dedication

from Upasarga अधि + Root 1046 √ इङ् अध्ययने । 2cA


1.3.1 भूवादयो धातवः । इङ्

1.3.3 हलन्त्यम् । 1.3.9 तस्य लोपः । इ

3.4.69 लः कर्मणि च भावे चाकर्मकेभ्यः । इ

3.2.123 वर्तमाने लट् । 3.4.77 लस्य । इ + लँट्

1.3.3 हलन्त्यम् । 1.3.9 तस्य लोपः । इ + लँ

1.3.2 उपदेशेऽजनुनासिक इत् । 1.3.9 तस्य लोपः । इ + ल्

3.4.78 तिप्तस्झिसिप्थस्थमिब्वस्मस् तातांझथासाथांध्वमिड्वहिमहिङ् ।

Atmanepada इ + तातांझ । conjugating third person

1.4.101 तिङस्त्रीणि त्रीणि प्रथममध्यमोत्तमाः ।

1.4.102 तान्येकवचनद्विवचनबहुवचनान्येकशः । इ + त । singular

1.4.108 शेषे प्रथमः । known as Prathma Purusha

3.4.113 तिङ्शित्सार्वधातुकम् । इ + त

3.1.68 कर्तरि शप् । 2.4.72 अदिप्रभृतिभ्यः शपः । इ + त

3.4.79 टित आत्मनेपदानां टेरे । इ + ते ।

1.2.4 सार्वधातुकमपित् । इ + ते । = इते <sup>लट् iii/1</sup> । She studies

    With Upasarga अधि + इते 6.1.101 अकः सवर्णे दीर्घः । =

अधीते <sup>लट् iii/1</sup> । She studies devotedly. She masters.

# Declension process of Noun

ललिता = Playful Goddess, Glow of Light, Sweet and Bright

Stem ललिता f → ललिता f 1/1

1.2.45 अर्थवदधातुरप्रत्ययः प्रातिपदिकम् । ललिता

1.2.46 कृत्तद्धितसमासाश्च । 3.1.1 प्रत्ययः । 3.1.2 परश्च ।

4.1.1 ङ्याप्प्रातिपदिकात्

4.1.2 स्वौजस-

मौट्छष्टाभ्याम्भिस्ङेभ्याम्भ्यस्ङसिभ्याम्भ्यस्ङसोसाम्ङ्योस्सुप् ।

1.4.104 विभक्तिश्च । 1.4.103 सुपः = use one of these vibhakti

suffix. ललिता + सुँ ।

1.4.22 ब्येकयोर्द्विवचनैकवचने = singular number taken.

ललिता + सुँ $^{1/1}$ ।

1.3.2 उपदेशोऽजननुनासिक इत् । 1.3.9 तस्य लोपः । ललिता + स् ।

6.1.68 हल्ङ्याब्भ्यो दीर्घात् सुतिस्यपृक्तं हल् । ललिता ।

= ललिता $^{f1/1}$ । *Feminine. First case singular.*

Playful Enchanting Charming Goddess. Attractive Light.
Delightful form. Evoking Sweetness. Giving Protection.

# Awadhi Alphabet अवधी

The Hanuman Chalisa is sung in Awadhi Language, connected to Ayodhaya, the land of Lord Ram. The Awadhi Alphabet was written in the Kaithi Script.

https://www.unicode.org/charts/PDF/U11080.pdf

Here we give the equivalent glyphs from the Devanagari script, as that is what is used in writing the Hanuman Chalisa today. The spoken Awadhi did not much use the letters which have been crossed out below.

अ आ इ ई उ ऊ ए ऐ ओ औ अं अः अँ

क ख ग घ ङ

च छ ज झ ञ

ट ठ ड ढ ण , additional letters with nukta ड़ ढ़

त थ द् ध न

प फ ब भ म

य र ल व

श ष स

ह

Note: Even if these letters are used,

The ष is usually pronounced as ख

The व is usually pronounced as ब

# References

https://www.ashtangayoga.info/philosophy/sanskrit-and-devanagari/transliteration-tool/
https://www.learnsanskrit.cc/

Shree Hanuman Chalisa by Gulshan Kumar, T-Series
https://www.youtube.com/watch?v=AETFvQonfV8
Hanuman Chalisa by Lata Mangeshkar, T-Series
https://www.youtube.com/watch?v=YPTfysi46io
Anirudh Tewari erstwhile Chief Secretary Punjab Govt, at Shri
Hanuman Mandir, Rajpura Road, Patiala
https://www.youtube.com/watch?v=n9LKYKkhkH0
Neem Karoli Baba - Hanuman Chalisa
https://nkbashram.org/hanuman-chalisa
Hanuman Chalisa chanting for World Peace, 2020
https://www.youtube.com/watch?v=G6E7U1BWZ0Y


227 – श्रीहनुमानचालीसा  - Gita Press, Gorakhpur.

Swami Rambhadracharya – श्रीहनुमान्-चालीसा (महावीरी व्याख्या सहित) –
4th – 2015 – Jagadguru Rambhadracharya Divyang
Vishvavidyalaya, Chitrakoot, UP.

Devdutt Pattanaik – मेरी हनुमान चालीसा  - 1st – 2018 – Rupa
Publications, New Delhi.

Swami Shivapadananda – Hanuman Chalisa of Goswami Tulsidas
- XXIst Reprint – 2010 – Sri Ramakrishna Math, Mylapore, Madras.

Swami Tejomayananda – Hanuman Chalisa - 1st – 2010 –
Chinmaya Prakashan, Mumbai.

S. K. Mutalik – Hanuman Chalisa of Tulsidasji   - 1st – 2004 –
Khemraj Shrikrishnadass, Bombay.
Baburam Saksena – Evolution of Awadhi   - 1st – 1938 – The Indian
Press, Allahabad.

# Epilogue

Sing freely.
Sing from your Soul.
Sing whenever you want.

Offer all to Him and rest deeply.

सर्वे भवन्तु सुखिनः । सर्वे सन्तु निरामयाः ।

सर्वे भद्राणि पश्यन्तु । मा कश्चिद् दुःख भाग् भवेत् ॥

ॐ शान्तिः शान्तिः शान्तिः ॥

When faith has blossomed in life,
Every step is led by the Divine.

Sri Sri Ravi Shankar

**Om Namah Shivaya**

जय गुरुदेव